MONEY
Doesn't Grow on
TREES

MONEY
Doesn't Grow on
TREES

And Other Financial Wisdom, Theories, Nostrums, and Outright Lies

BRECK SPEED
AND
MARK DUTTON

CUMBERLAND HOUSE

Nashville, Tennessee

Published by Cumberland House Publishing, Inc., 2200
Abbott Martin Road, Suite 102, Nashville, Tennessee 37215.

Jacket design by Bruce Gore, Gore Studios
Page design by Julie Pitkin
Illustrations by Vic Harvell

Distributed to the trade by
Andrews and McMeel
4900 Main Street
Kansas City, Missouri 64112

Library of Congress Cataloging-in-Publication Data

Speed, Breck, 1956
    Money doesn't grow on trees : and other examples of
financial wisdom, theories, nostrums, & outright lies / Breck
Speed & Mark Dutton.
        p.   cm.
    ISBN 1-888952-17-2
    1. Investments—Quotations, maxims, etc.   2. Finance—
Quotations, maxims, etc.   3. Stocks—Quotations, maxims,
etc. I. Dutton, Mark, 1960-   II. Title.
HG4528.S668   1996
332—dc20   96-32181
                                                             CIP

Printed in the United States of America
1 2 3 4 5 6 7 8—00 99 98 97 96

To
the Greater Fools
who have bailed us out
on several occasions

Introduction

*S*ooner or later, most of us find some great cause to champion. You know, something like a cure to cancer. World peace. Religious harmony. Or a really good nacho cheese dip that won't clump. All of these worthy boals have eluded humankind (or at least the folks in my neighborhood) since time immemorial.

My personal Holy Grail is an equally mythical and seemingly unattainable goal: the perfect investment strategy. By that I mean a system of investment that results in better than average returns—maybe even an occasional home run—with zero risk. That's not too much to ask in return for the use of my money by a total stranger, is it? Man has already reached the moon. All I'm asking is to beat the Dow Jones Industrial Average consistently.

I've been on this quest for most of my adult life. Shortly after I embarked on it, I realized I needed serious help. After all, I was young, inexperienced, and—even worse—a lawyer. In other words, I knew next to nothing of practical consequence in the business world except how to sue a corporation and how to perfect a security interest. Even if I somehow stumbled on a perfect investment system, I thought, how would I ever recognize it on my own? I needed a mentor.

A mentor soon appeared in the form of Mark Dutton. Mark was—and is—a loyal friend, confidant, stockbroker of the highest order, and scratch golfer. He was younger than I, but since all those business types kept trusting him with their money, I figured he had learned a lot for his years. If nothing else, maybe he could help me with my golf swing.

Dutton foolishly agreed to help me, and we started our search by asking ourselves the following questions: How do the financial wizards make all that money? Do successful investors and businessmen know something the rest of us don't understand? Is it necessary to inherit wealth like a Rockefeller or cheat like a Milken? Could we distill the wisdom of the ages from the countless financial journals, newspapers, books, television shows, radio programs, and private newsletters? Could we get a tip in the eighth race at Oaklawn?

It didn't take long before we realized we had begun a journey that would involve a great deal of work and might take years to complete. For more than a decade, we searched for reliable insights and an honest buck, plumbing the mysteries of the international financial markets and everyday business world. Using my legal and business training, I worked the streets through the mud and muck, daily searching for that guru who could enlighten me. Ink from volumes of financial journals stained my hands. My eyesight dimmed. Weeks would pass without any clues or new leads. And yet I slogged on doggedly.

Meanwhile, Dutton worked the phones and stayed dry.

I don't want to whine, but "buy low, sell high" sounds great until you actually have to do it. Also iff we get another chance on this earth, I want to come back as a stockbroker.

Did we find the Grail, the one perfect investment strategy? Well ... no. But we did discover a host of interesting, if not entirely valid, maxims. A maxim is a complete thought shrunk to one or two sentences. A lot of the maxims we discovered are "moldy oldies." A few appear to be new thoughts. Seriousness and humor appear side by side.

This book records our passage from near total ignorance to, well ... near total ignorance. Unfortunately, we have to admit that our exhaustive research did not get me—or anyone else—closer to the goal of the perfect investment strategy. Hey, we tried, but none of the maxims we discovered were foolproof. And besides, if I had discovered the perfect investment strategy, do you think I'd be telling the general public?

However, we did determine that the investment world has a lot of truly intelligent people, all trying to find the same perfect investment strategy. They come from a host of educational, business, and professional backgrounds and, naturally, have an almost limitless variety of theories on how to be successful in business and finance. The entirely predictable result is a hodge-podge of maxims that more or less contradict one another. In fact, probably the most accurate law of investment states that the opposite of an investment rule—if applied consistently—works as well as the rule itself. If that isn't confusing! Perhaps a variation of one of Einstein's laws of physics applies best: For every action (read, "maxim") there is an equal and opposite reaction (read, "loss of capital").

In the final analysis, all we can offer you is our sincere wishes for good fortune. We had great fun collecting this anthology of investment philosophy, and we hope you find it enjoyable reading. May I suggest in the bathroom? Next to the fancy towels, perhaps. Discovery of the Holy Grail will have to wait for more serious minds.

—Breck Speed

*T*ake advantage of
what you already know.

*I*nvest your time
before you invest your money.

A free market economy,
like nature, abhors a vacuum.

*W*all Street is the only place
to which people ride in a Rolls Royce
to get advice from those who
take the subway.

A study of economics reveals
that the best time to buy anything
is usually last year.

*I*f a government robs Peter
to pay Paul, it can rely upon
the support of Paul.

*I*f you're in the grocery business,
don't sell what you wouldn't eat.

You can marry more money in five minutes
than you can earn in a lifetime.

*T*he time to buy a straw hat
is in the Fall.

*N*o one ever bet too much money
on a winning horse.

*T*he best money is
made on fear.

*T*he best way to make money
is to have other people
make it for you.

*T*rading financial futures is only
slightly more risky than feeding
your cash directly to pigs.

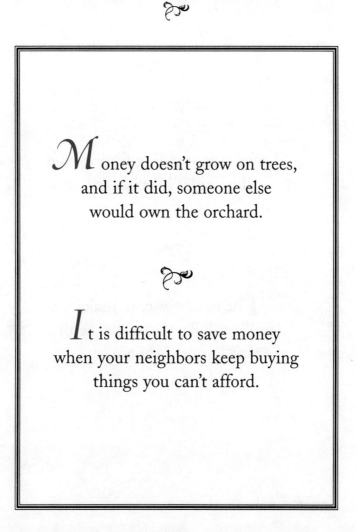

*M*oney doesn't grow on trees,
and if it did, someone else
would own the orchard.

*I*t is difficult to save money
when your neighbors keep buying
things you can't afford.

*N*ever buy anything from a man
who jingles his change.

*T*he easiest way to make
a million dollars is to start with
nine hundred thousand.

❧

$\mathcal{M}$ost people do not realize
that there's just as much money to
be made when a society is falling
down as when it's rising up.

❧

$\mathcal{T}$he stock market can only do what
the bond market allows.

A businessman is like a turtle.
He gets nowhere unless he sticks
his neck out.

A man who owns little
is little owned.

I nvestor confidence
is a perishable commodity.

A bull market
climbs a wall of worry.

*I*f it quacks like a duck,
walks like a duck, and looks like
a duck, most likely it is a junk bond.

*F*irms that view bad times
as bad times are inclined towards
inaction, and inaction in bad times
is very expensive.

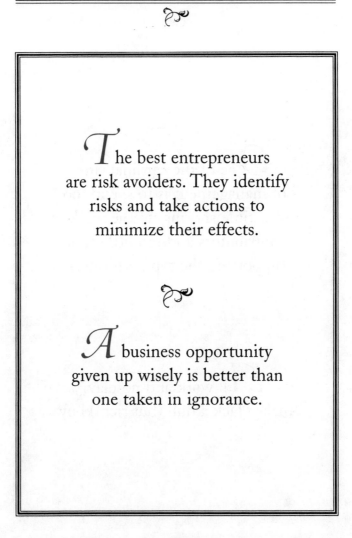

*T*he best entrepreneurs
are risk avoiders. They identify
risks and take actions to
minimize their effects.

A business opportunity
given up wisely is better than
one taken in ignorance.

*O*ne of the cardinal sins
of management is to spend too
much time shoring up the weakest
contributors and too little time
supporting the top performers.

*A*ll work and no play
makes Jack a dull (but rich!) boy.

I ncomes are like shoes.
If your income is too small,
it pinches you; and if it is too large,
it causes you to stumble and trip.

P overty is nothing to be
ashamed of, but it is to be gotten rid
of as soon as conveniently possible.

The road to success
is always under construction.

*I*f the investment waters
are muddied, don't jump in.

*T*rade not—want not.

*I*nvestors never think in crowds—
investors think alone.

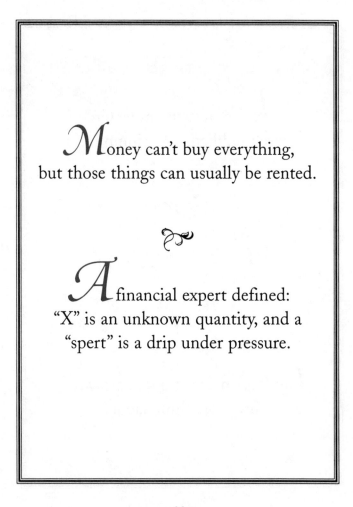

$\mathcal{M}$oney can't buy everything,
but those things can usually be rented.

$\mathcal{A}$ financial expert defined:
"X" is an unknown quantity, and a
"spert" is a drip under pressure.

❧

A banker is a friend who lends
you an umbrella, then asks for it back
when it looks like its going to rain.

❧

*T*he problem of overdiversification:
If you have a harem of forty women,
you never get to know any of
them very well.

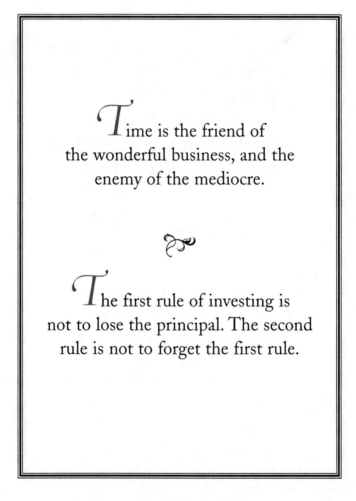

*T*ime is the friend of
the wonderful business, and the
enemy of the mediocre.

*T*he first rule of investing is
not to lose the principal. The second
rule is not to forget the first rule.

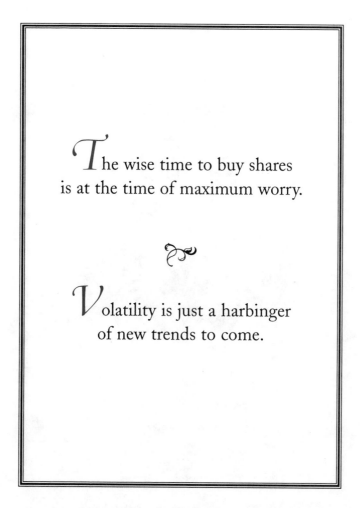

*T*he wise time to buy shares
is at the time of maximum worry.

*V*olatility is just a harbinger
of new trends to come.

Creditworthiness is next
to godliness.

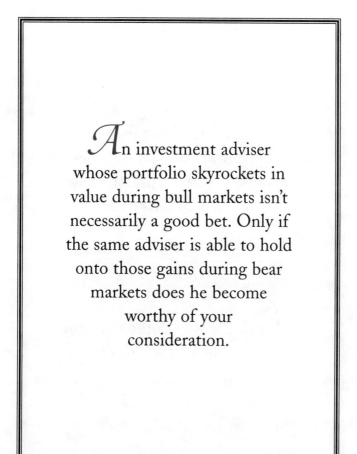

*A*n investment adviser whose portfolio skyrockets in value during bull markets isn't necessarily a good bet. Only if the same adviser is able to hold onto those gains during bear markets does he become worthy of your consideration.

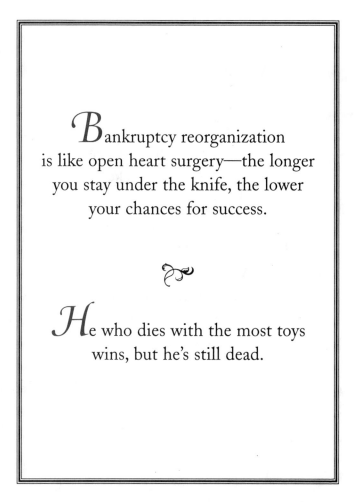

*B*ankruptcy reorganization
is like open heart surgery—the longer
you stay under the knife, the lower
your chances for success.

*H*e who dies with the most toys
wins, but he's still dead.

Never ask a lawyer or an
accountant for business advise.
They are trained for find problems,
not solutions.

The big print giveth, and the
small print taketh away.

In seeking investments,
opportunities rather than security
should be the driving force. After all,
a boat in a harbor is safe, but in time
its bottom will rot.

The deal's not done until
the check has cleared the bank.

ॐ

*C*apital to be invested
is like a beautiful woman.
It has a lot of suitors.

ॐ

*T*he "Cockroach Theory"
of investing assumes that when
one bad earnings report shows up,
another will follow it.

Bad times are great for morticians.

*D*on't reinvent the wheel.

*T*he average investor is always wrong.

*B*uy low, sell high.

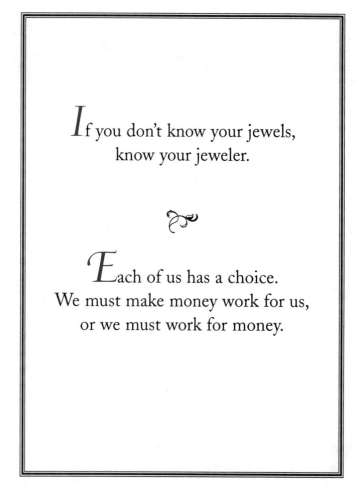

*I*f you don't know your jewels,
know your jeweler.

*E*ach of us has a choice.
We must make money work for us,
or we must work for money.

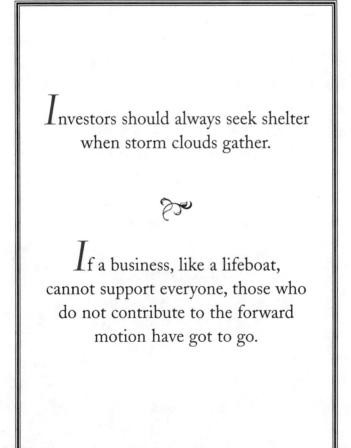

*I*nvestors should always seek shelter
when storm clouds gather.

*I*f a business, like a lifeboat,
cannot support everyone, those who
do not contribute to the forward
motion have got to go.

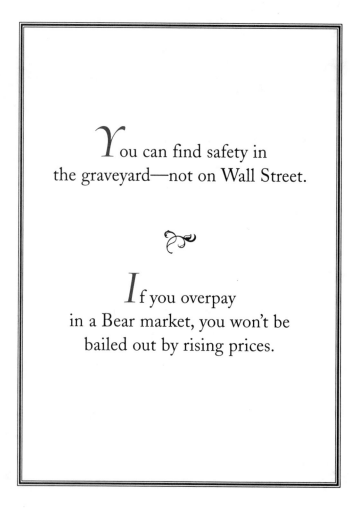

You can find safety in
the graveyard—not on Wall Street.

If you overpay
in a Bear market, you won't be
bailed out by rising prices.

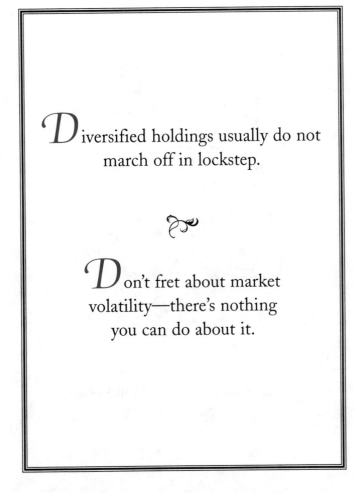

*D*iversified holdings usually do not march off in lockstep.

*D*on't fret about market volatility—there's nothing you can do about it.

If you want a friend on Wall Street,
buy a dog.

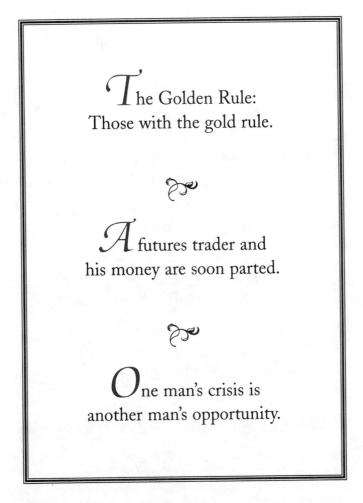

*T*he Golden Rule:
Those with the gold rule.

A futures trader and
his money are soon parted.

*O*ne man's crisis is
another man's opportunity.

*S*afety is owning stock in companies that you would be comfortable owning if the stock market shut down for five years. You wouldn't need to worry they might go out of business.

*M*amas, don't let your babies grow up to buy tax shelters.

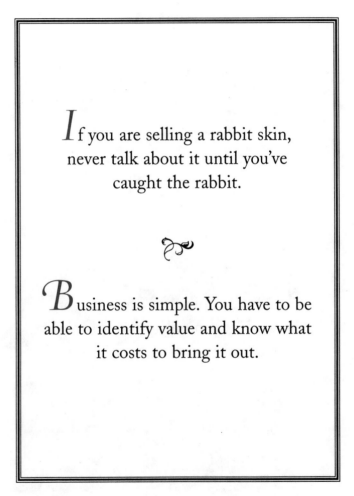

*I*f you are selling a rabbit skin,
never talk about it until you've
caught the rabbit.

*B*usiness is simple. You have to be
able to identify value and know what
it costs to bring it out.

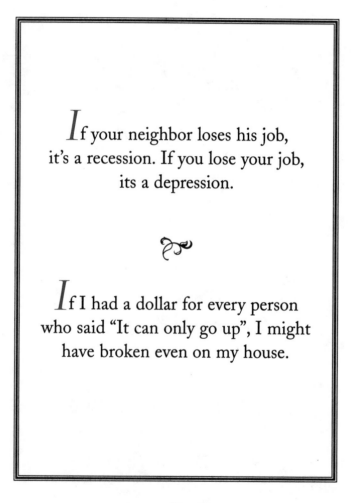

*I*f your neighbor loses his job,
it's a recession. If you lose your job,
its a depression.

*I*f I had a dollar for every person
who said "It can only go up", I might
have broken even on my house.

❧

*F*inding a great short sell
is easy—all you need to do is get
hold of a list of a brokerage firm's
favorite "buy" recommendations.

❧

*H*e who sells what isn't his'n
buys it back or goes to pris'n.

Cheap stuff tends to get cheaper.

*P*overty follows greed.

*A*nyone can own a new car
for thirty days.

*N*ever let success go uncopied.

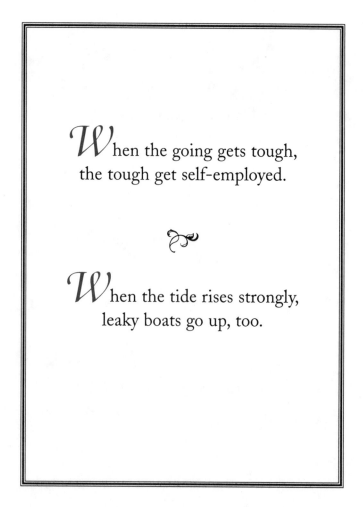

*W*hen the going gets tough,
the tough get self-employed.

*W*hen the tide rises strongly,
leaky boats go up, too.

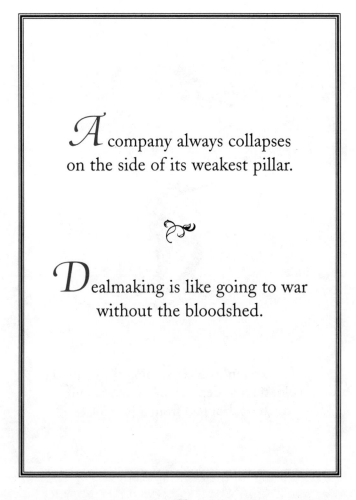

A company always collapses
on the side of its weakest pillar.

*D*ealmaking is like going to war
without the bloodshed.

If a "recession" is like catching the common
cold, then a "depression" is like catching
an anvil dropped from a high place.

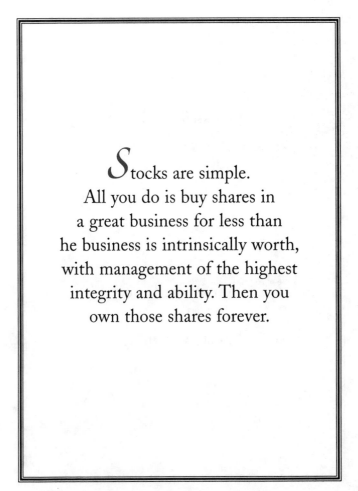

Stocks are simple.
All you do is buy shares in
a great business for less than
he business is intrinsically worth,
with management of the highest
integrity and ability. Then you
own those shares forever.

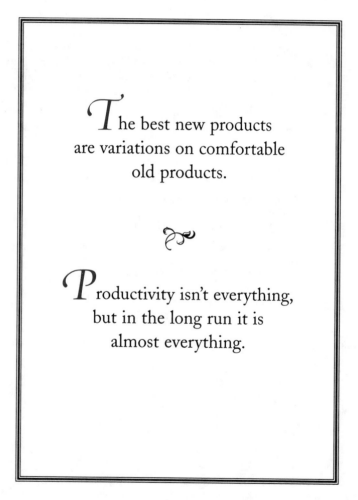

The best new products
are variations on comfortable
old products.

Productivity isn't everything,
but in the long run it is
almost everything.

There are two types of economists:
Those who don't know the future,
and those that don't know that
they don't know the future.

Beware the naked man
who offers you his shirt—he's
trying to sell you a book.

*I*n a leveraged society,
only cash can make your
dreams come true.

*S*uccess in investing,
as in life, requires balance.

*I*f you want to get
yourself better off financially,
quit buying things.

*I*ndustry, perseverance,
and frugality make fortune yield.

Nothing encourages creative thinking
in quite the same way as poverty.

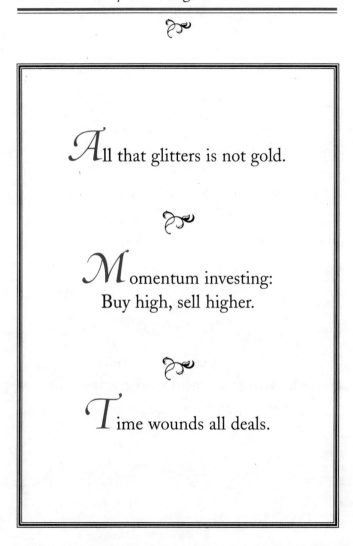

All that glitters is not gold.

Momentum investing:
Buy high, sell higher.

Time wounds all deals.

*D*on't try to make a killing
on short-term market moves;
they are impossible to predict
with accuracy.

*T*he art of bottom-fishing
is knowing when to stop cutting bait
and when to start casting your line.

*N*o one has ever made money
panicking, although fortunes have
been made by those who induced
others to panic.

*I*n times of crisis,
there is a flight to quality
and a flight to lunacy.

*W*hen the market becomes conservative, as it does in times of unrest, the speculative issues are the ones most likely to suffer.

*I*t is easier to buy a company than it is to sell it.

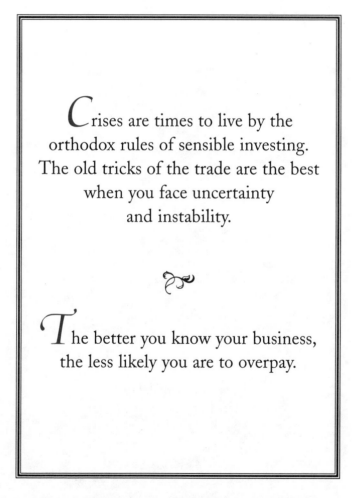

*C*rises are times to live by the
orthodox rules of sensible investing.
The old tricks of the trade are the best
when you face uncertainty
and instability.

*T*he better you know your business,
the less likely you are to overpay.

If you don't make dust
in your business, you eat it.

*R*ob the train
before you split up the loot.

*W*ork works.

*Y*ou gotta have a gimmick.

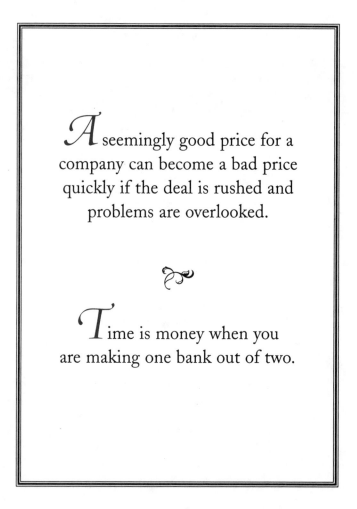

A seemingly good price for a company can become a bad price quickly if the deal is rushed and problems are overlooked.

*T*ime is money when you are making one bank out of two.

*I*t is one thing to buy a business and another thing to manage it.

*T*he most important three factors for a real estate project are location, location, and location.

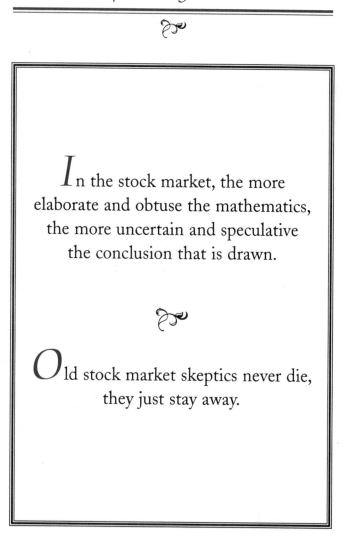

*I*n the stock market, the more elaborate and obtuse the mathematics, the more uncertain and speculative the conclusion that is drawn.

*O*ld stock market skeptics never die, they just stay away.

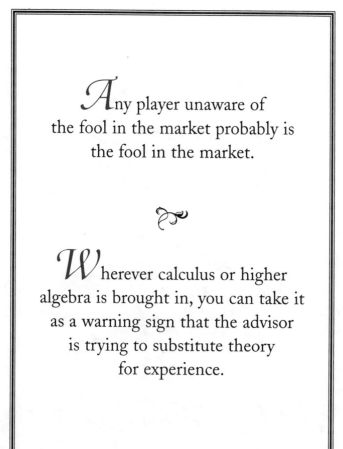

*A*ny player unaware of
the fool in the market probably is
the fool in the market.

*W*herever calculus or higher
algebra is brought in, you can take it
as a warning sign that the advisor
is trying to substitute theory
for experience.

You have to kiss a lot of frogs
to find a prince.

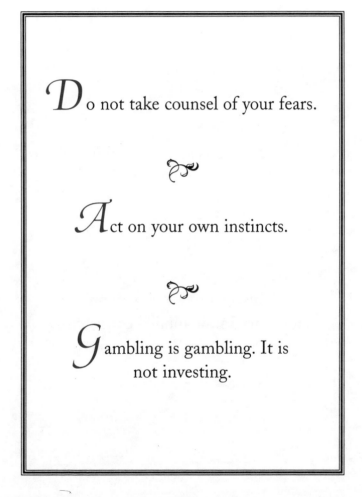

*D*o not take counsel of your fears.

*A*ct on your own instincts.

*G*ambling is gambling. It is not investing.

❧

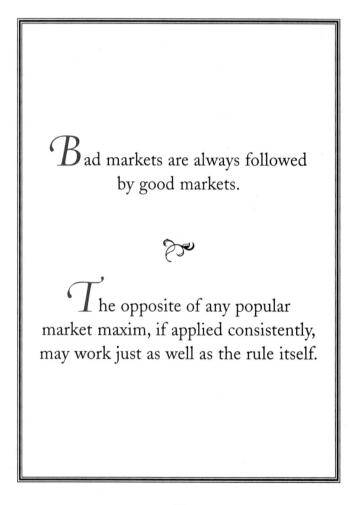

*B*ad markets are always followed
by good markets.

❧

*T*he opposite of any popular
market maxim, if applied consistently,
may work just as well as the rule itself.

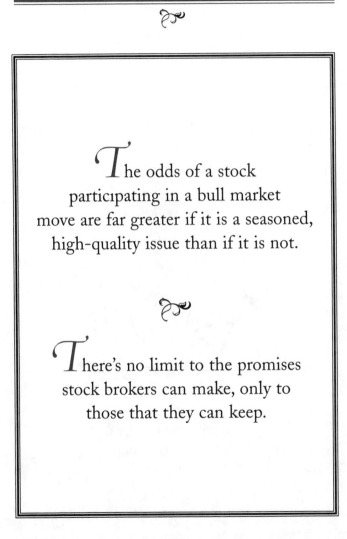

*T*he odds of a stock participating in a bull market move are far greater if it is a seasoned, high-quality issue than if it is not.

*T*here's no limit to the promises stock brokers can make, only to those that they can keep.

Run with the big dogs,
or whine with the puppies.

*T*he common denominator of
all successful investors, encompassing
many different approaches to the
market, is their ability to curb
destructive emotions and instead
employ the productive emotions
of patience, confidence, and
long term resolve.

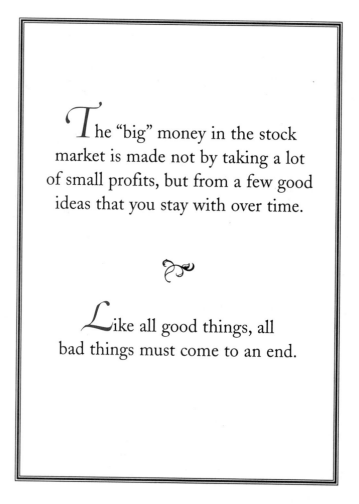

*T*he "big" money in the stock market is made not by taking a lot of small profits, but from a few good ideas that you stay with over time.

*L*ike all good things, all bad things must come to an end.

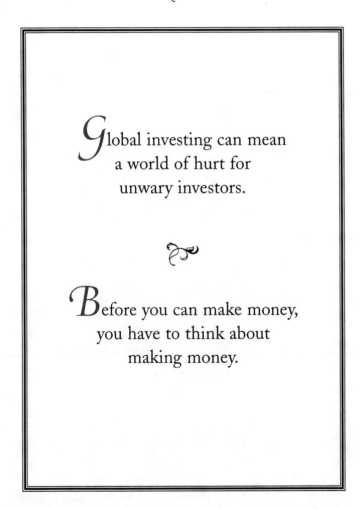

*G*lobal investing can mean
a world of hurt for
unwary investors.

*B*efore you can make money,
you have to think about
making money.

*B*e everywhere, do everything,
and never fail to astonish
the customer.

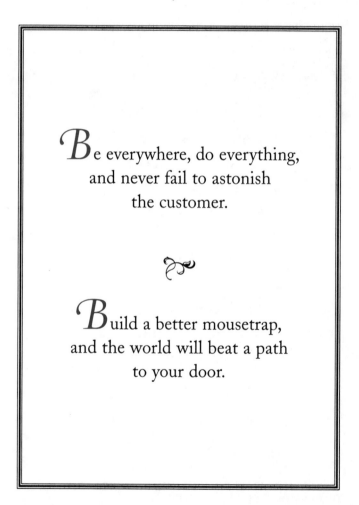

*B*uild a better mousetrap,
and the world will beat a path
to your door.

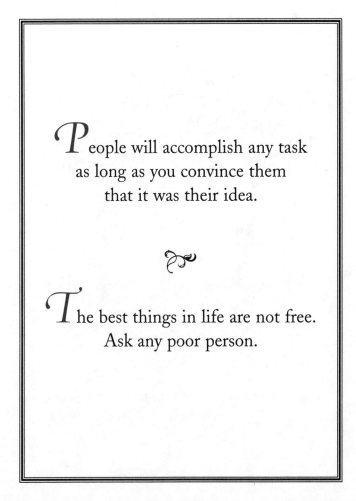

*P*eople will accomplish any task
as long as you convince them
that it was their idea.

*T*he best things in life are not free.
Ask any poor person.

Wall Street's graveyards are filled with people
who were right too soon.

༂

*T*he difference between economists and finance experts lies in how they would determine the market price of ketchup. The economist would look at the price of tomatoes, wages, and ketchup substitutes. The finance expert would observe that a two-quart bottle of ketchup costs twice what a one-quart bottle did, say the market was efficient, and leave it at that.

*E*very piece of property is worth something, even if it's nothing more than keeping the sunlight out of hell.

*T*he man who reads the morning paper for the likely results of his speculative investments makes himself unfit for calmly considering how to solve the day's business problems.

*T*he volume of share
sold on the stock exchanges
is directly related to the volume
of rumors circulating
on Wall Street.

*B*oth Bulls and Bears
can make money in the market,
but Hogs get slaughtered.

*I*nnovations in the financial market are subject to the Iron Law of Unintended Consequences.

*A*ll great stock pickers with long term records got that way by staying stock pickers.

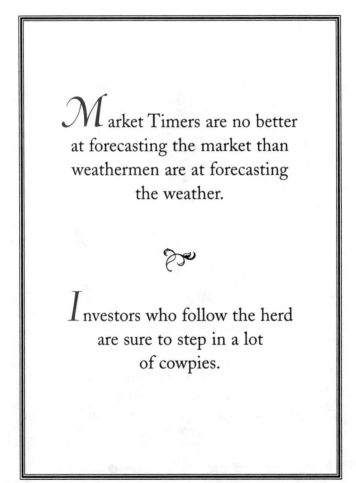

*M*arket Timers are no better
at forecasting the market than
weathermen are at forecasting
the weather.

*I*nvestors who follow the herd
are sure to step in a lot
of cowpies.

Buying more stock in a losing position
to lower your cost is like running under a safe
that someone dropped from a building
to try and break its fall.

Don't fall in love with
your investments.

No boom—no bust.

Buying begets more buying.

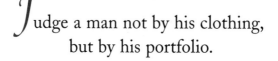

*J*udge a man not by his clothing,
but by his portfolio.

*M*arvelous stories have
been told about how well leveraged
buy outs and takeovers have worked,
but anyone who has been in debt
has a different outlook—debt is
something you have to repay.

❧

*W*hen the public is clamoring
for stocks, the top of the market
is usually near.

❧

*T*rade for the short term
because in the long term we'll
all be dead.

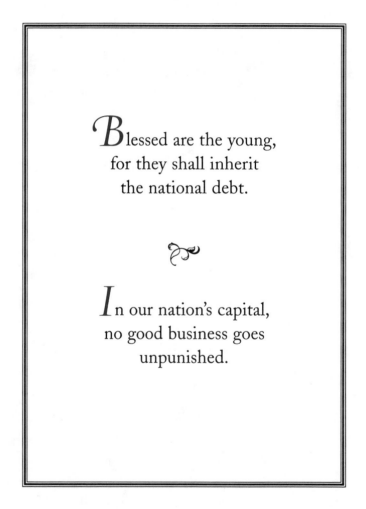

*B*lessed are the young,
for they shall inherit
the national debt.

*I*n our nation's capital,
no good business goes
unpunished.

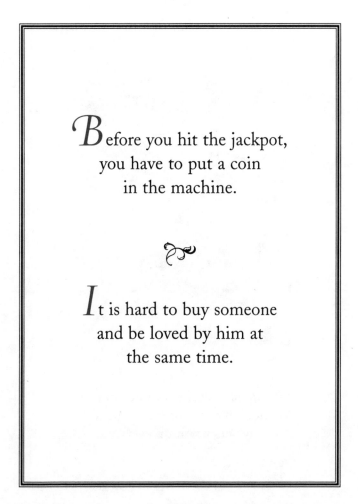

*B*efore you hit the jackpot,
you have to put a coin
in the machine.

*I*t is hard to buy someone
and be loved by him at
the same time.

Insurance salesmen profit on fear.
Stock brokers profit on greed.
Lawyers profit on everyone.

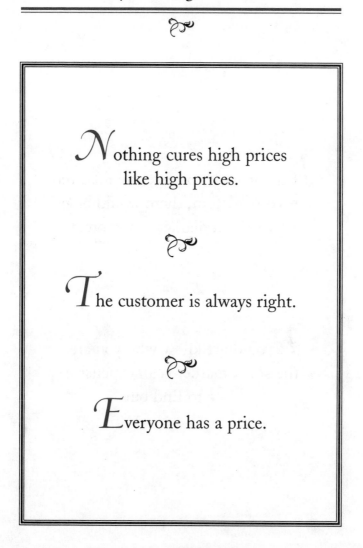

*N*othing cures high prices
like high prices.

*T*he customer is always right.

*E*veryone has a price.

*I*f the market consistently followed the same pattern, there would be no two-sided markets anymore.

*I*f you don't know who you are, the stock market is an expensive place to find out.

❧

*S*tock market crashes come and go,
but politics last forever.

❧

*M*arkets gravitate to one set of
numbers or another because investors
are always searching for a clue
to market behavior.

*I*f you lined up all the
economists in the world end-to-end,
they still would not reach a conclusion.

*I*t is not hard to do something smart
in the market. Think of something
dumb, and do the opposite.

❧

*Y*ou must be able to take your losses
as well as your wins.

❧

*I*n time, investors who
cut through the emotional
blocks and weigh probabilities
will beat those who play it safe.

How well the investors do on a
leveraged buy out is a function of
how badly they screw the banks.

*T*he greater the risk,
the greater the reward.

*B*usiness succeeds when it
sweats the small stuff.

*I*n the 1980s, a good time
was had by some.

Beware of a buyer
who says price does not
matter, for he does not
intend to pay you.

Beware of the seller who
will sign a warranty without an
argument, for he does not
intend to honor it.

If enough layers of management have superimposed on one another, you can be assured that disaster has not been left to chance.

If all persons calling themselves investment advisers were piled on top of each other, beginning at the bottom of the Grand Canyon, it probably would be a good idea.

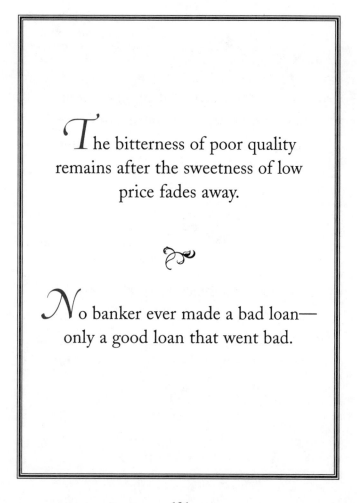

*T*he bitterness of poor quality remains after the sweetness of low price fades away.

*N*o banker ever made a bad loan— only a good loan that went bad.

❧

*J*ust as there are some things
that money can't buy, there are some
problems that money can't solve.

❧

*B*ull markets die with a whimper,
not with a bang.

If one thing is predictable,
it is that the market is unpredictable.

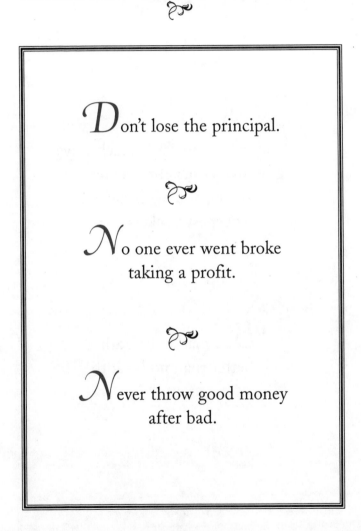

$\mathcal{D}$on't lose the principal.

$\mathcal{N}$o one ever went broke
taking a profit.

$\mathcal{N}$ever throw good money
after bad.

The market moves in such ways
that it always benefits the fewest
participants with the
deepest pockets.

Bad market breadth
is better than no breadth
at all.

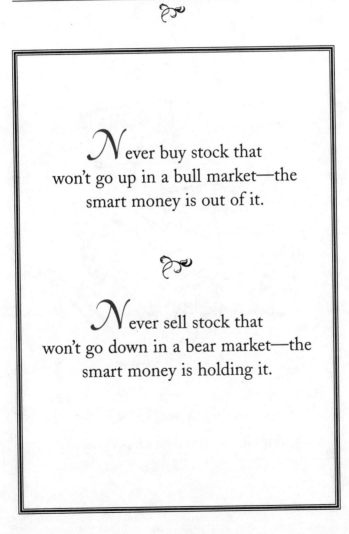

*N*ever buy stock that won't go up in a bull market—the smart money is out of it.

*N*ever sell stock that won't go down in a bear market—the smart money is holding it.

You can't sell from an empty wagon.

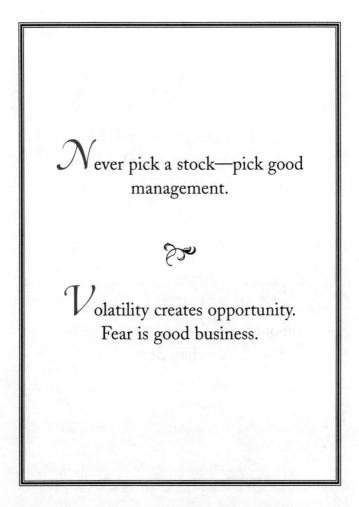

Never pick a stock—pick good management.

Volatility creates opportunity. Fear is good business.

A company with no debt
on its balance sheet will find it
very difficult to go bankrupt.

*W*hen all is said and done
about financial analysts, more is
said than done.

The most expensive four words on Wall Street are "This Time It's Different."

If you hold your losers and take profits on your winners, you'll end up with a portfolio of losers.

*I*t is better that a deal
should fail on Wall Street than
go bust on Main Street.

*W*hen trading spreads,
lifting one leg of the spread often
exposes your soft parts.

꙰

A "deal driven" market
is like a lottery, in that all tickets
(or stocks) go up in value because of
the possibility of more big winners
being drawn.

꙰

T he beauty of the market is
that when excesses develop, at some
point you get a crash.

Life insurance is only good if it is in force when you die.

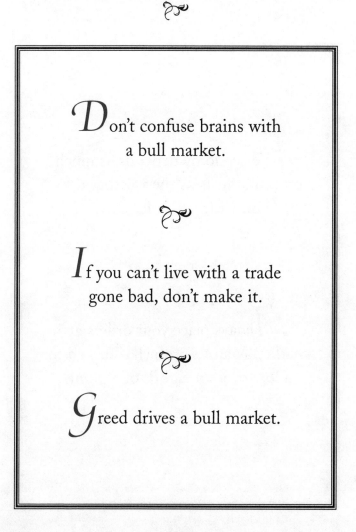

*D*on't confuse brains with
a bull market.

*I*f you can't live with a trade
gone bad, don't make it.

*G*reed drives a bull market.

*T*he economy depends as much
on economists as the weather does
on weather forecasters.

*A*lways place your orders at
market. Many a profit has turned to
a loss over an eighth of a point.

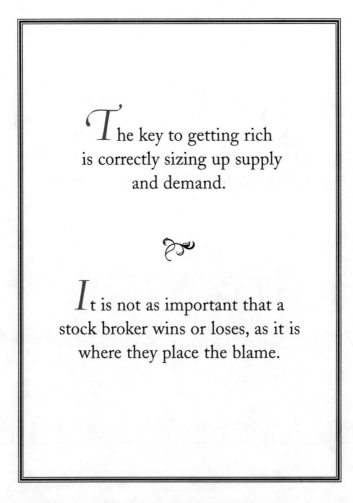

*T*he key to getting rich
is correctly sizing up supply
and demand.

*I*t is not as important that a
stock broker wins or loses, as it is
where they place the blame.

*O*ptimists make more money than pessimists, but pessimists never need to scale back their expectations.

*T*here is no greater pariah on Wall Street than company that fails to sell itself.

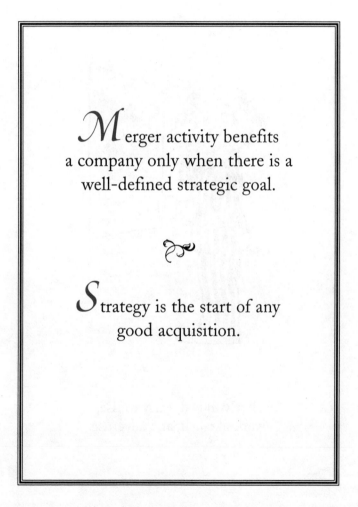

$\mathcal{M}$erger activity benefits
a company only when there is a
well-defined strategic goal.

$\mathcal{S}$trategy is the start of any
good acquisition.

Early to bed, early to rise,
work like hell, and advertise.

❧

*A*n entrepreneur is someone
who takes a prospective hire out
into the country to a hill overlooking
a great estate; points to the mansion,
swimming pool, stables, and tennis
courts; and says, "If you come
with me and work your butt
off, someday all of this
will be mine."

*N*o matter what the other attributes are of a deal, if you overpay, it's a bad deal.

*B*eware the "Cadillac Spread"— you lose in a up-move, you lose in a down-move, but the stockbroker who sold you the spread drives a Cadillac.

*T*here are three ways to
lose money: a woman is the most
pleasurable; gambling is the fastest;
and farming is the surest.

*I*f you would know
the value of money, try to
borrow some.

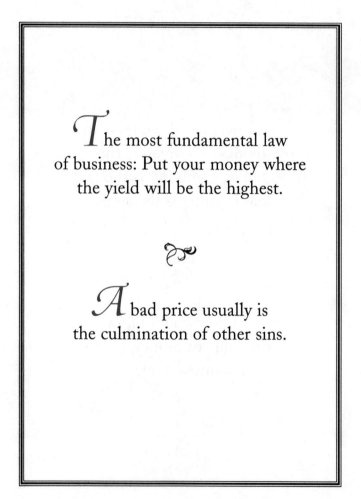

*T*he most fundamental law
of business: Put your money where
the yield will be the highest.

A bad price usually is
the culmination of other sins.

❧

*A*n investment banker
is just a pawnbroker with
an imagination.

❧

*T*he only value of
stock forecasters is to make
fortunetellers look good.

Profits are like breathing—if you
don't breathe, you're dead.

*P*ros average up; suckers average down.

*I*f you must profit on this trade, you will lose.

*D*on't fight the tape.

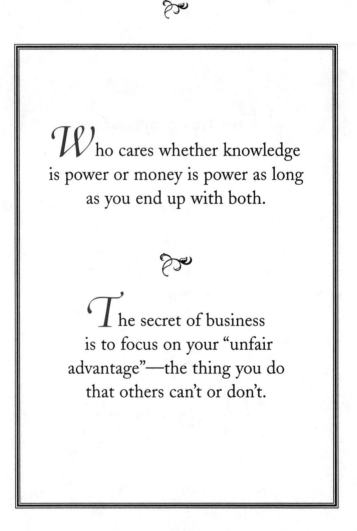

*W*ho cares whether knowledge is power or money is power as long as you end up with both.

*T*he secret of business is to focus on your "unfair advantage"—the thing you do that others can't or don't.

*T*he first rule of management:
If enough people meet often enough,
for a long enough period of time, they
will eventually plan something
that can't be done.

*T*he way to become an entrepreneur
is one sale at a time.

The market will go through corrections, but if you pick the right stocks they'll act like tennis balls and not eggs.

Nothing ruins a bargain so much as getting what you paid for.

❧

*I*f starting a business was easy,
everyone would do it, and then there
would be no money in it.

❧

*B*usiness is like sex.
When it's good it's wonderful,
and when it's bad it's still
pretty good.

If you can't buy lemons, you
can't sell lemonade.

$\mathcal{L}$ife insurance isn't purchased
—it's sold.

$\mathcal{T}$he surest way to prosperity
is to earn it.

$\mathcal{A}$void investment clichés
like the plague.

*M*ind your pennies,
and the dollars will mind
themselves.

*M*oney isn't everything,
but it sure keeps you in touch
with your children.

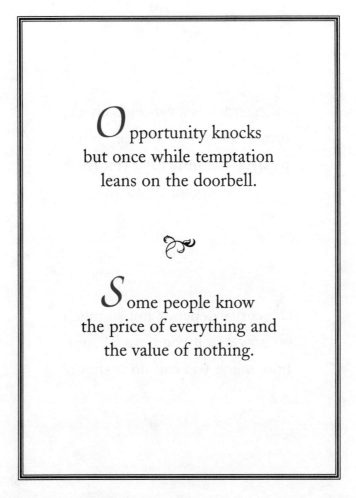

*O*pportunity knocks
but once while temptation
leans on the doorbell.

*S*ome people know
the price of everything and
the value of nothing.

❧

Υesterday is a canceled check;
tomorrow is a promissory note;
today is the only cash you have
—so spend it wisely.

$\mathcal{S}$ecurity depends not so much
on how much you have as upon
how much you can do without.

*I*f you ever wondered who
the "powers that be" are—they
are the powers that will be
writing the checks.

*W*hen you are down and out,
something always turns up—and it is
usually the noses of your "friends."

None of the secrets of success will work
unless you do.

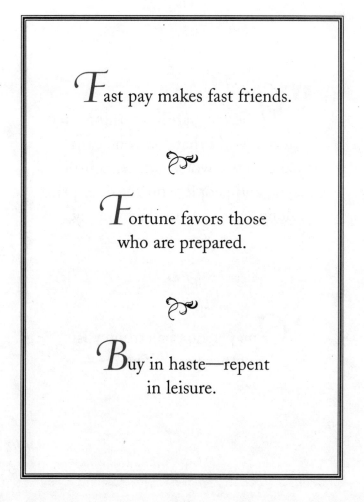

*F*ast pay makes fast friends.

*F*ortune favors those
who are prepared.

*B*uy in haste—repent
in leisure.

*T*here is hardly anything
in the world that someone can't
make a little worse and sell a little
cheaper, and people who consider price
alone are this man's lawful prey.

*O*ne person's bankruptcy is
another person's gain.

*T*he common law
of balance prohibits paying a
little and getting a lot.

*W*hen the company announces
a new corporate headquarters,
sell its stock.

*T*he best thing about money
management is that it is indoor work
with no heavy lifting.

*T*he race isn't necessarily
to the swift, but that's the
way to bet it.

❧

*N*obody is smarter
than the guy who gave you
the last winner.

❧

*N*one of the old rules
work any more—but then
they never did.

Don't become a seller of buggy whips.

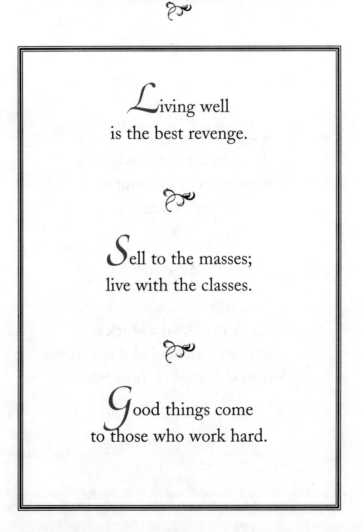

*L*iving well
is the best revenge.

*S*ell to the masses;
live with the classes.

*G*ood things come
to those who work hard.

*Y*ou can't trust newly rich
management or anyone in
investor relations.

*N*ever own a stock if
the corporate title includes the words
Universal, Global, or *Intergalactic.*

❧

*T*here are many millionaires
on Wall Street, not all of whom
started out as multimillionaires.

❧

*T*here are no atheists in foxholes,
nor conservatives when the subsidies
are being passed out.

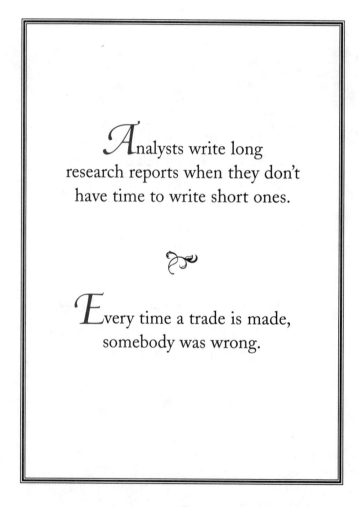

*A*nalysts write long
research reports when they don't
have time to write short ones.

*E*very time a trade is made,
somebody was wrong.

*T*here is more than one way to skin a cat and six ways to roll a seven.

*D*on't ask your legal or tax counsel "if" but "how."

If you open a burger stand,
don't try to be McDonald's, or
you'll get your butt kicked.

A penny saved
will depreciate rapidly.

*T*he stock doesn't know you own it.

*T*o err is human, to hedge divine.

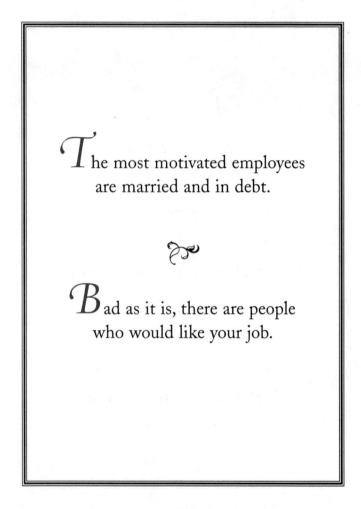

*T*he most motivated employees
are married and in debt.

*B*ad as it is, there are people
who would like your job.

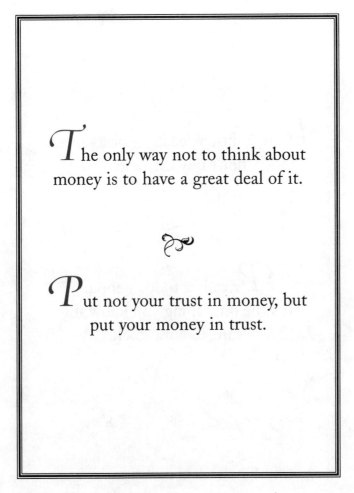

*T*he only way not to think about money is to have a great deal of it.

*P*ut not your trust in money, but put your money in trust.

*I*f the industry leader is overvalued,
don't buy the dogs.

*P*rice is a fundamental.
It's the only thing you know for
sure about a stock.

*D*on't bet on a sure thing unless you can afford to lose.

*B*uy anything that's worth four dollars and costs one dollar.

Bull markets tops are driven by
"Greater Fools." During this period,
no matter what you buy, you can always
sell at a profit to a Greater Fool.

$\wp$

$\mathcal{Y}$ou've never met a rich pessimist.

$\wp$

$\mathcal{B}$ears don't live in mansions.

$\wp$

$\mathcal{T}$he trend is your friend.

*H*ighly successful businesses
and highly paid executives
seldom intermingle.

*T*he employer generally gets
the employees he deserves.

$\mathcal{W}$ork like you'll
live forever; play like you'll
die tomorrow.

$\mathcal{T}$he richer a salesman
hopes to make you, the faster
you should run.

Υou can't do today's job
with yesterday's tools and expect
to be in business tomorrow.

$\mathcal{G}$overnment is run like
nobody's business.

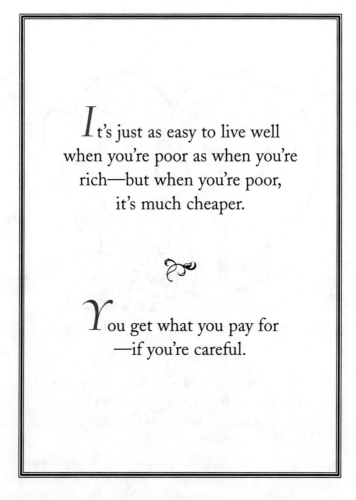

*I*t's just as easy to live well
when you're poor as when you're
rich—but when you're poor,
it's much cheaper.

*Y*ou get what you pay for
—if you're careful.

If they're selling elephants two for a quarter,
it's a great bargain, but only if you have a
quarter and need two elephants.

*H*e who rides the horse
of greed at a gallop will pull it
up at the door of shame.

*P*rice is what you pay,
and value is what you get.

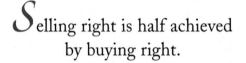

*S*elling right is half achieved
by buying right.

*T*he best time to sell a stock
is when there is some better use
for your money.

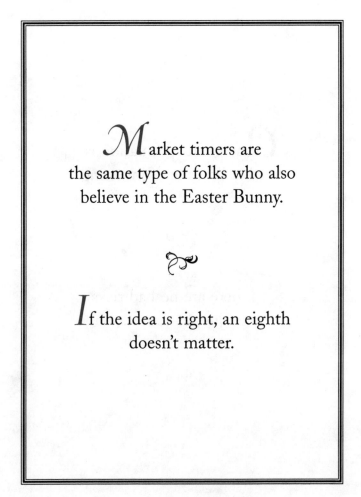

$\mathcal{M}$arket timers are
the same type of folks who also
believe in the Easter Bunny.

$\mathcal{I}$f the idea is right, an eighth
doesn't matter.

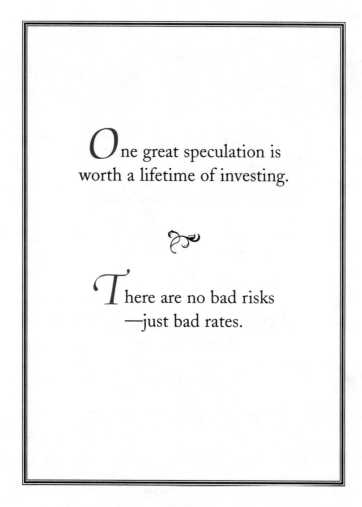

*O*ne great speculation is worth a lifetime of investing.

*T*here are no bad risks —just bad rates.

❧

*I*f you want to see a short month,
sign a thirty-day note.

❧

*M*anaging what you owe
is as important as managing
what you own.

Forget about the fat lady singing
—it isn't over until the check
clears the bank.

*W*hat you don't own
can't hurt you.

*P*eople who buy stocks
when they get bonuses and sell
them when their car breaks down are
entrusting their investment
decisions to their cars.

*C*ompound interest is the
eighth wonder of the world.

*N*ever take another man's bet.
He wouldn't offer if he didn't know
something you don't.

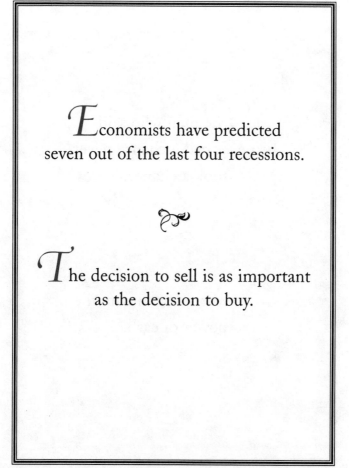

*E*conomists have predicted
seven out of the last four recessions.

*T*he decision to sell is as important
as the decision to buy.

*T*he man who said
he never had a chance never
took a chance.

*N*ever underestimate the
power of cash.